Accounting Essentials

Managing by the Numbers

Jay Jacquet

50-Minute Manager™

Accounting Essentials
Managing by the Numbers

Jay Jacquet

CREDITS:

VP, Product Development:	**Charlie Blum**
Editor:	**L.K. Woodbury**
Assistant Editor:	**Genevieve McDermott**
Design:	**Nicole Phillips**
Production Artist:	**Rich Lehl**

ISBN 10: 1-56052-698-X
ISBN 13: 978-1-56052-698-8
Library of Congress Catalog Card Number 2005922700
Printed in the United States of America
4 5 6 11 10 09

Learning Objectives for

ACCOUNTING ESSENTIALS

The objectives for *Accounting Essentials* are listed below. They have been developed to guide the user to the core issues covered in this book.

The objectives of this book are to help the user:

1) Learn how various business transactions are reflected in the financial statements

2) Identify the five cost categories and their components

3) Explore the three types of costs and their effect on profitability

4) Understand the concept and calculation of break-even analysis

5) Learn about operating leverage and its impact on profitability

6) Discover the various influences on determining the appropriate price for a product or service

7) Understand the problem-solving process of identifying costs relevant to decision-making

ASSESSING PROGRESS

A 50-Minute Manager™ assessment is available for this book. The 25-item, multiple-choice and true/false questionnaire allows the reader to evaluate his or her comprehension of the subject matter.

To download the assessment and answer key, please visit *www.logicaloperations.com/file-downloads* and search by course title or part number.

Assessments should not be used in any employee selection process.

About the Author

Jay L. Jacquet has taught business and accounting courses for more than 25 years at numerous universities in Ohio and has consulted with many businesses on technical issues. He currently teaches as adjunct faculty with three universities and is CEO of his own firm, Educational Consulting Services.

Jay holds a B.B.A., Business Education, and an MBA from the University of Toledo and is a licensed public accountant. He continues to consult, write, and provide accounting services.

Preface

Business runs by the numbers. This book was written to help explain the relationships among numbers and how they affect decision-making. The one question managers and customers are always asking is:

What is this going to cost me?

It is important to understand terms related to costing products and services. Then it is important to understand how costs relate and build on each other. Finally, it is important to understand the impact costs have on your decisions.

Accounting Essentials is about understanding the impact of financial data on day-to-day operations. Managers today cannot leave financial decision-making to the accounting or financial departments only. All involved must understand:

➤ The cost of their product or service

➤ The price strategies

➤ The impact that short- and long-term decisions have on the bottom line

Understanding more about financial decision making should enable you to communicate effectively throughout your organization. This book will introduce you to how financial data is collected, allocated, and used within your organization.

Please pay careful attention to the examples and complete the self-tests in the Appendix. Enjoy the process.

Introduction

Decision-making is key to every aspect of a business. Whether you are in your own business or working for someone else, you will make a variety of decisions every day. The ability to respond effectively to decision-making conditions requires quantitative information. A better understanding of how to use these numbers in the basic functions of business will lessen the risk associated with a decision.

Management consists of five basic functions:

> Control

> Lead

> Organize

> Plan

> Staff

Accounting Essentials is about decision-making in relation to the control function. Two basic objectives of this function are to create efficient and effective processes within the organization. To determine whether the company is efficient and effective, the organization needs a report card. This report card is based on numbers, numbers, and more numbers.

Most of the financial information for the external and internal users in your company is historical data. But decision-making is about looking into *tomorrow*. Decisions into tomorrow require formats other than classic financial statements. Reorganizing this information will provide many answers to questions you may have raised with your associates. The objective is to get you asking more questions and understanding the "whys" and "ways" that numbers affect process.

Table of Contents

PART 1

Getting the
"Right" Numbers

Qualitative vs. Quantitative Decision-Making

Let's say you are thinking about purchasing a new car. There are two kinds of decisions you will need to make. One requires quantitative data—such as information about price, car payments, miles per gallon, and the manufacturer's maintenance history. The other kind of decision requires qualitative information such as color, interior material, seat comfort, and so on. The difference between the two is defined as follows:

> ➤ Quantitative decision-making should be *capable of measurement*.

> ➤ Qualitative decision-making is simply *information that is not quantifiable*.

Although both of these methods can be important to your decision, *Accounting Essentials* emphasizes the use of quantitative data. The quality, efficiency, and effectiveness of decision-making require the use of numbers to measure progress.

Management must make the best decision using all the tools available. Many of the numbers may be soft (within a range) and involve other non-quantifiable alternatives. Remember, the more solid the numbers calculated, the less risk involved in that decision.

Standards

A key question in every organization is "How do we measure progress?" The response to this question is in the data provided, such as:

- ➤ **Profit or loss**—"the bottom line" related to net income or loss
- ➤ **Growth**—increase in market share
- ➤ **The return on investment (ROI)**—percent of return on investment
- ➤ **The "right" cost for the product or service**—cost to deliver goods and services to the customer
- ➤ **Increase in sales**—continued growth by selling more product

These items require numbers to help answer the question of progress. Data alone will not answer all the questions. Today, with databases and computer-integrated systems, there is an increased ability to capture a great deal of information. All of this financial information must be put into usable formats.

The importance of maintaining consistency of information in financial statements for managerial decision-making cannot be overstated. Many businesses have gotten into serious financial trouble from management's failure to respond to internal or external quantitative information or simply to ask the "right" questions.

Remember, one of the major functions of management is to establish control. A large part of the control process requires, especially with today's global competition, being efficient and effective. To be efficient and effective, an organization must establish standards.

A standard is a measure of adequacy.

Management can set very high standards or low ones. Standards become the benchmarks for you to measure success or failure. Standards can be obtained through your own and others' experience and the analysis of technical processes. Other control methods are available in every business. Examples of these are:

- ➤ Budgets
- ➤ Financial reports
- ➤ Observations
- ➤ Control charts and graphs
- ➤ Ratios (comparisons and relationships among numbers)

The numbers drive all of these methods.

Effective and Efficient Decisions

Remember, a major role of management is to create processes that are both *efficient and effective*. Let's define what is meant by these terms:

> **Efficient**—the ability to produce a product with a minimum of effort or expense

> **Effective**—the ability to produce a desired or definite result

It would be difficult to prove a process is efficient or effective without using numbers. These numbers need to be accurate, timely, and consistent.

Accurate	2+2=4
Timely	
Consistent	Procedures are the same from period to period

Failure to follow these guidelines will create unusable information.

Caveats (Beware!)

This book has been written using generally applied cost principles and terminology. Others within your business may collect, analyze, and distribute the financial information. Some of the processes and allocation of costs may not be the same in your company. But no matter what system of data collection is used, the numbers and the methods for getting those numbers should be explained to those who need them. The first step in making sure that we have the right numbers is for everyone to understand how we got the numbers.

Keep an open mind while learning the processes used in this book. These methods may be different from company to company. The basic tools used here are a starting point. It is equally important when using quantitative information that you understand how the number is calculated and how it relates to other numbers. Ask questions. Management has a responsibility to use the financial information for internal decision-making. This responsibility requires an understanding of financial and management reports generated within your company.

Constraints

Every organization has constraints. Management's responsibility is to provide resources (where possible) to ease these constraints. The organization must continuously deal with the following limitations:

> Money

> Capacity

> People

These constraints are major concerns for any business. Other constraints may appear in production systems such as bottlenecks, backorders, and downsizing production personnel. This stretching and shrinking of the production environment and other constraints are a continual challenge for managers. The purpose of "good" data is to aid the manager in providing solutions to these constraints and furthering cost reduction and containment. Before major changes in costs are implemented, the following question must be answered:

What impact does this change or reduction in cost have on the process?

Very few costs work in isolation from each other. There are process links between customer and product. Reduction of costs without considering process can create a deadly mix resulting in loss of customers. Production personnel must understand the reasons for cost containment and aid in making sure improved process results from these changes. Cutting costs alone may lead to loss of quality and customer dissatisfaction.

PART 2

Review of the Financial Statements

The Balance Sheet and Income Statement

It is important to have a basic understanding of the financial statements and reports used in your company. This section is not meant to cover everything you need to know about these statements but to serve as a review of the fundamentals. More information can be obtained by reading the book, *The Accounting Cycle*, by Jay Jacquet.

All transactions in an accounting system will have an impact on two or more accounts.

These accounts can be classified into one of five categories used throughout the system. The five categories are:

- Assets
- Liabilities
- Equity
- Revenue
- Expenses

Examples of accounts in each of the five categories are shown in the following table:

Assets	Liabilities	Owner's Equity	Revenue	Expenses
Cash Accounts Receivable Inventory Equipment Buildings Land	Accounts Payable Notes Payable	Capital Contributions Withdrawals **OR** Common Stock Additional Paid in Capital Capital **AND** Retained Earnings	Sales Interest Earned	Wages Rent Depreciation Advertising Utilities

These five categories are combined to create two important financial statements: the *balance sheet* and the *income statement*.

➤ Balance sheet accounts include assets, liabilities, and equity

➤ Income statement accounts include revenue and expenses

The Balance Sheet

Assets = Liabilities + Owner's Equity

$100,000 = $49,000 + $51,000

The purpose of the balance sheet is to provide the financial "position" of the company on a specific date, such as December 31, 2004.

The Income Statement

		July	August
	Revenue	$1,000	$1,500
Less:	Total Expenses	850	1,750
=	Net income or (loss)	$150	$(250)

The purpose of the income statement is to provide profit and loss from operations. This is usually done month to month, such as for the month ended July 31, 2004.

Let's illustrate how various transactions can affect the two financial statements. These are the transactions:

1. Invested $10,000 in the business

2. Made sales of $400 on account +S asset expense, liabilities

3. Paid the rent, $300

4. Purchased a building for $25,000 and land for $3,000 with $5,000 cash and the remainder on credit

5. Made sales and received cash of $600 A/R

6. Purchased $5,000 of equipment on credit

7. Paid wages of $500

8. Received a utility bill for $150 A/P

Now let's see which categories each of these transactions falls in to. Remember, the five categories for accounts are:

Assets	Liabilities	Owner's Equity	Revenue	Expense

1. 2004 Invested $10,000 in the business.

Because the $10,000 is your own money, this transaction increases cash and capital.

Assets	Liabilities	Owner's Equity	Revenue	Expense
Cash +10,000		Capital +10,000		

2. Made sales of $400 on account

This is revenue. The company earned it even though it was not paid, and because it was not paid, it is placed in accounts receivable (A/R).

Assets	Liabilities	Owner's Equity	Revenue	Expense
A/R +400			Sales +400	

3. Paid the rent of $300

This is an expense paid in cash.

Assets	Liabilities	Owner's Equity	Revenue	Expense
Cash -300				Rent expense -300

4. Purchased a building for $25,000 and land for $3,000 with $5,000 cash and the remainder on credit.

This is a complicated transaction, but notice that the difference in the assets (25,000 + 3,000 -5,000) falls into the liability category as a note payable.

Assets	Liabilities	Owner's Equity	Revenue	Expense
Buildings +25,000 Land +3,000 Cash -5,000	Notes payable +23,000			

5. Made sales and received cash of $600

In this transaction the company was paid for a job completed.

Assets	Liabilities	Owner's Equity	Revenue	Expense
Cash +600			Sales +600	

6. Purchased $5,000 of equipment on credit.

The company borrowed money to purchase equipment.

Assets	Liabilities	Owner's Equity	Revenue	Expense
Equipment +5,000	Notes payable +5,000			

7. Paid wages of $500

Paid company employees' wages

Assets	Liabilities	Owner's Equity	Revenue	Expense
Cash -500				Wage expense -500

8. Received a utility bill for $150

Received the bill but it is not yet paid.

Assets	Liabilities	Owner's Equity	Revenue	Expense
	Accounts payable +150			Utility expense -150

A summary of the transactions follows:

Balance Sheet

Assets		=	Liabilities		+	Owner's Equity	
Cash	$4,800		Accounts Payable	$150		Capital $10,000	
A/R	$400		Notes Payable	$28,000			
Equipment	$5,000						
Building	$25,000						
Land	$3,000						
Totals	$38,200	=		$28,150	+		$10,000
					+	Income	50
							$10,050

Note: The balance sheet—$38,200 = 28,150 + 10,000—does not balance. The balance sheet will not balance until net income or loss is included in owner's equity. Once the $50 of income (see the following income statement) is added to owner's equity, the assets of the company—$38,200—will equal the liabilities—$28,150 plus owner's equity of $10,050.

Income Statement Transactions

Revenue:

Sales (transaction 2)	$400
Sales (transaction 5)	600
Total Sales	$1,000

Expense:

Rent expense (transaction 3)	$300
Wage expense (transaction 7)	500
Utilities expense (transaction 8)	150
Total Expenses	950
Net Income (sales – expenses)	**$50**

The Income Statement will be used throughout this book. This statement is a collection of company revenues and expenses for a period of time—usually one month.

Income Statement

Revenue from sales and services			$1,000
Less Expenses:	Wage Expense	$500	
	Rent Expense	300	
	Utilities Expense	<u>150</u>	
			<u>950</u>
Net income			**$50**

Statement of Cash Flow

To understand the purpose of the *Statement of Cash Flow*, you must first understand the difference between two accounting systems: the accrual system vs. the cash system. The separate cash flow analysis, which the statement of cash flow represents, is important to companies that operate on the accrual system.

With the cash system, income and expenses are recorded when money changes hands. Someone pays you for a service and you record that as revenue. You pay for office supplies and you record that as an expense.

The Accrual System of Accounting

In most accounting systems, revenue is recorded at the time the service is performed or the product is sold, and expenses are recorded at the time they are incurred, regardless of when the money actually changes hands. This is the *accrual system*.

Because revenue and expenses are not the same as cash, external reporting requires that a Statement of Cash Flow accompany the income statement. This statement reflects all transactions in cash. The purpose of this statement is to explain the difference in the cash account from one year to the next on the balance sheet.

A large non-cash expense to be reflected in the Cash Flow Statement is depreciation, which is a method of expensing large assets such as buildings, equipment, and autos. Accounting standards require that a major asset be expensed over its useful life rather than all at once at the time of purchase.

Example: Truck Cost $$\frac{\$25,000}{5 \text{ years (useful life)}} = \$5,000 \text{ depreciation per year}$$

The depreciation per year is not cash. It is an expense on your income statement but does not require any cash payment. Therefore, it must be added back to net income on the cash flow statement.

The Cash Flow Statement generally consists of:

Cash from operations	Begin with:	Net income (the "bottom line")
	Add:	Depreciation of assets
	Adjust for:	Sales not received in cash (A/R)
		Expenses not paid in cash (A/P)
		Inventory purchases

Note that the adjustments for A/R, A/P and Inventory may be deductions or additions depending on the change in the account balance from the prior year. For instance, if A/R is higher than the prior year, you have received less of your sales in cash, and that is a deduction. In contrast, if A/P is higher than the prior year you have used less of your cash for expenses, and that is an addition.

Cash from investments	Add:	Cash from sales of long-term assets (Property, plant, equipment, securities)
	Deduct:	Cash used to purchase long-term assets
Cash from financing	Add:	Cash from sales of company stock Proceeds from long-term debt
	Deduct:	Cash used to repurchase company stock Cash used to repay long-term debt

A simple example shows the difference that can exist between cash flow and income as reported under the accrual system. This illustration is for J.D. Lawn Service with the following information taken from the balance sheet and income statements provided.

J.D. Lawn Service
Balance Sheet
September 30, 20XX

Assets		Liabilities & Equity	
Cash	$ 5,000	Accounts Payable	$ 300
Accounts Receivable	3,500	Notes Payable	15,000
Inventory	1,000	Total Liabilities	$15,300
Truck and Trailer, net	13,500		
Mowing Equipment, net	12,300	J.D. Capital	$20,000
Total Assets	$35,300	Total	$35,300

J.D. Lawn Service
Income Statement
For Months July, August, September

<u>Revenue</u>

Grass cutting $37,000

<u>Expenses</u>

Wage expense	$14,800	
Gasoline	1,480	
Maintenance	296	
Supplies	925	
Truck depreciation	1,200	
Equipment depreciation	1,200	
Telephone expense	262	
Advertising expense	3,145	
Administrative services	1,020	
Utilities expense	370	
Rent expense	2,400	
Miscellaneous expense	1,850	
Total Expenses		$28,948
Net Income or (Net Loss)		$8,052

[handwritten: $2,400 Depreciation bracketing the Truck depreciation and Equipment depreciation entries]

The following is a simple example of a partial cash flow statement. J.D. Lawn Service had no cash transactions from investment or financing activities. Notice the cash from operations is not the same as the net income figure on the Income Statement. This difference can be substantial when companies do not collect revenue quickly and have large amounts of depreciation from equipment.

J.D. Lawn Service
Cash Flow Statement
For July 1–August 31

Cash from operations:

Net income		$8,052
Add:		
	Depreciation	2,400
	Increase in A/P*	300
Deduct:		
	Increase in A/R**	3,500
Total Cash from Operations		$7,252 ← **Difference $800**
Net Income from the Income Statement		$8,052

* A $300 bill for advertising was received at the end of the month. The Balance Sheet shows the account payable of $300. The advertising expense on the income statement shows $3,145 was purchased, but because only $2,845 was actually paid in cash, this $300 account payable must be added to net income on the cash flow statement. The cash has not yet been paid out.

** Grass cutting revenue is reduced by $3,500 because the Balance Sheet shows an Account Receivable indicating this cash revenue has not yet been received.

What the Financial Statements Do Not Tell You

The goals of an organization are often expressed in its mission statement. The mission statement is a direct result of goals and objectives prepared each year. To achieve these goals, the organization needs financial resources, people, and daily processes. The ability of management to plan, control, and direct operational activities is affected by the financial statements.

Management must work with the providers of financial information and request the proper data to judge the company's progress.

Management should be able to answer:

- ➤ How well is the organization doing financially?

- ➤ Is the company financially viable for the present and the future?

- ➤ Is the company being effective and efficient?

- ➤ How does the customer view the organization?

- ➤ How well is the organization creating new markets?

The management team must be concerned with the cost effectiveness of its business processes as well as production procedures. And management must continually monitor the needs and satisfaction levels of its customers.

The numbers on the financial statements are like a golf score. At the end of 18 holes you may have shot a score of 92. But this number does not explain how many drives you flubbed or how many iron shots it took or the number of putts. The score does not answer the basic question of how to correct your various high scores and fix your game. It takes practice and patience and the ability to work through the problems. The numbers will help you. Likewise, looking at each of the various financial statements and their relationship with one another will help you fix your company.

Using J.D Lawn Services as an example, we'll see where to look for company problems. Accomplishing this task calls for examining and reorganizing the financial information for J.D. Lawn Services. Let's get started!

The following Income Statement for J.D. Lawn will be used throughout the book to illustrate the concepts of each objective.

J.D. Lawn Service
Income Statement
For Months July, August, September

	July	August	Sept	Total
Revenue:				
Grass cutting	$12,000	$10,000	$15,000	$37,000
Expenses:				
Wage Expense	$ 4,800	$ 4,000	$ 6,000	$14,800
Gasoline	480	400	600	1,480
Maintenance	96	80	120	296
Supplies	300	250	375	925
Truck Depreciation	400	400	400	1,200
Equipment Depreciation	400	400	400	1,200
Telephone Expense	86	84	92	262
Advertising Expense	1,020	850	1,275	3,145
Administrative Services	340	340	340	1,020
Utilities Expense	120	100	150	370
Rent Expense	800	800	800	2,400
Miscellaneous Expense	600	500	750	1,850
Total Expense	$ 9,442	$ 8,204	$11,302	$28,948
Net Income or (Net Loss)	$ 2,558	$ 1,796	$ 3,698	$ 8,052

] $2,400

Making Money

Maximizing Profit or Minimizing Cost

Before knowing *if* your company is making money, you need to know *how* to make money. There are three ways to produce a more profitable business:

➤ **Increase sales:** Sell more units, increasing total sales and producing more income.

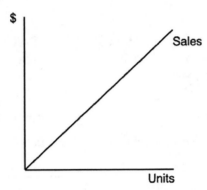

➤ **Decrease costs:** Reduce the costs of products or services, providing more profit for the company.

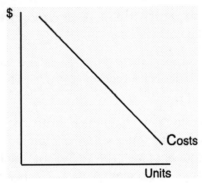

➤ **Increase sales and decrease costs:** Sell more units *and* reduce the costs of products or services, resulting in a more profitable position for the company

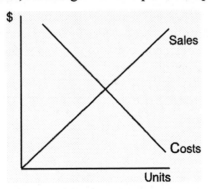

Let's look at a simple example of increasing sales or decreasing costs. Company A and B have the same sales and expense figures.

	Company A	Company B
Sales	$1,000,000	$1,000,000
Expenses	950,000	950,000
Profit	$ 50,000	$ 50,000

Management wants to increase net profit from $50,000 to $100,000. To do so, Company A decides to increase marketing (resulting in increased sales) while Company B decides to reduce costs.

	Company A		Company B	
Sales	$2,000,000	(was $1,000,000)	$1,000,000	
Expenses*	1,900,000		900,000	(was $950,000)
Profit	100,000		100,00	

*This problem assumes that expenses will increase proportionally with sales, although this is not always the case.

Company A had to exert considerable effort, doubling sales to achieve the desired results. But Company B merely reduced expenses by 5.26% (rounded) to achieve the same result.

This simple model compels you to think about the objective of either increasing sales or decreasing costs. Doubling the sales volume requires a great deal of activity. Reducing expenses requires some "belt tightening" and looking for efficiency within the organization. The reduction of 5.26% in costs produces the same profit result.

The above example illustrates the importance of looking at costs along with thinking about increasing sales. Not all costs increase proportional to sales. When business is good and sales are strong, there is less pressure to cut costs. When business downturns occur, however, cost containment and reduction become requirements to maintain a competitive edge.

Thinking in Units

As we begin to think about costs, it makes sense to reduce the numbers to a size that can be grasped. It is easier to imagine drinking eight, 8-oz. glasses of water a day than a 64-oz. jug of water. The same is true when considering financial information.

Governments are well-known for using large numbers that are difficult to understand. Let's say the village of Fairfield wants to pass a tax for $2 million to collect refuse weekly. This number does not have much significance to individuals because it is large and difficult to grasp. But if the $2 million is divided by the number of households in the village and the number of weeks of pickup service, the cost comes out to $15 per household per week.

$$\frac{\$2,000,000}{2,565 \text{ residents}} = \$780 \text{ per year}$$

$$\frac{\$780}{52 \text{ weeks}} = \$15 \text{ per week for refuse collection}$$

This figure takes on a meaning citizens can grasp. They can look at how much refuse the average person in the village discards and the cost per 30-gallon container, or some other standard. This results in data people can use. Village management and customers now have some idea of the cost per household and can make decisions using these costs.

The village may ask:

➤ Do we stay with city collection or outsource to a private carrier?

➤ Is this cost too high or low?

The same concept can be applied to a retail company with sales of $10 million. This is only a large number. It does not explain whether the company's prices are too high or perhaps not high enough. The number begins to take on meaning, however, when the company sees that it is selling 40,000 units at $250 per unit.

It is important to look at sales and costs per unit. Collection of information other than a dollar figure will provide additional perspective to decision making. The number alone can be deceiving. The following inventory data is a good example of deception.

Example:

	Year	Inventory
A retail company:	2003	$1,200,000
	2004	2,400,000

Looking at the inventory number, you might assume the company has more inventory on hand. But additional information on units and cost reveals:

	Units	Cost per Unit
Inventory 2003	60,000	$20.00
Inventory 2004	50,000	$48.00

Inventory costs have skyrocketed! And there are fewer units.

Do not make hasty assumptions about an increase or decrease of revenue and costs. The number of units and cost per unit will help greatly in decision making.

Defining Cost

Exactly what do we mean by the word cost? In financial accounting the term *cost* refers to the use of cash or other resources. The machine cost $300 or the utility bill cost $150.

The cost terms below are used in different ways. These costs are associated with different purposes.

Before identifying costs and their behaviors and other classifications, it is important to understand the terminology associated with these costs. Costs can be classified into the following categories.

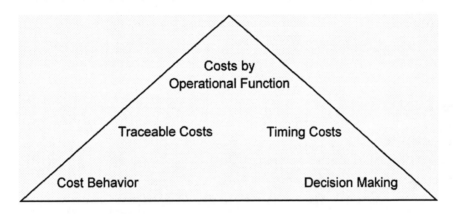

Let's look at each classification and define terms that make up each one.

Operational Function

Manufacturing costs:

Direct Material	*All materials that become a part of the product*
Direct Labor	*Labor that directly makes the product*
Factory Overhead	*Indirect material, labor, and other costs in manufacturing*

Non-manufacturing costs:

Cost of goods sold	*Finished inventory ready to sell*
Administrative expenses	*All expenses in administration*
Marketing expenses	*All expenses to sell product*

Traceable Costs

Direct Costs:

Direct Material	*Trace materials directly to the product*
Direct Labor	*Trace labor directly to the product*

Indirect Costs:

Factory overhead	*These costs are not directly related to the product*
Common costs	*These costs are related to the process but not specific product*

Timing Costs

Product Costs:

Inventory costs	*Inventory on hand such as raw material, work in process inventory, and finished good inventory*

Period Costs:

Marketing expenses	*Charged against revenue for the same period of time*
Administrative expenses	*Charged against revenue per month*

Cost Behavior

Variable Costs	*Costs that change with volume of activity*
Fixed Costs	*Costs which do not change with volume of activity*
Mixed Costs	*A cost with both fixed and variable elements*

Decision-Making Types of Costs

Standard Costs	*Predetermined costs budgeted*
Sunk Costs	*Costs that have already been incurred—these are past costs*
Opportunity Cost	*Loss of income from rejecting one alternative for another*
Relevant costs	*Costs that differ between alternatives*

From a control and planning management operational view, the most important of these classifications is cost behavior which changes with volume of activity.

Identifying Costs
and Their
Behaviors

Fixed, Variable, and Mixed Costs

All business expenses can be classified into one of three areas: variable expenses, fixed expenses, or mixed (both variable and fixed). These costs have a relationship to volume. The more volume, the more costs incurred, although this is generally not true for fixed costs. This section defines these costs and looks at their relationship to volume.

Total Fixed Costs

Fixed costs are expenses that do not change with volume; they remain the same no matter what the volume. Examples of fixed costs include:

➤ Rent expense

➤ Depreciation expense

➤ Car lease

➤ Equipment rental

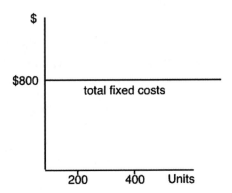

Total refers to units times dollars. For fixed costs, the expense totals each month are *not* affected by the volume of the product or service produced. As the number of units increases, there is no change in the fixed cost.

Total Variable Costs

Variable costs are expenses that change with volume. Examples of variable costs include:

> ➤ Wage expense (hourly or piece-rate employees)

> ➤ Material used in production of a product

> ➤ Gasoline and other supplies to service the equipment

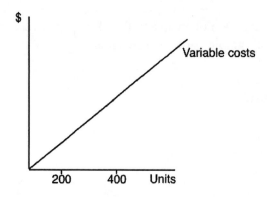

Again, *total* refers to units times dollars. For variable costs, the expense totals will change with volume. As the units produced increases, the total variable cost to produce the units continues to increase.

Total Mixed Cost

Mixed costs have elements of fixed and variable expenses, so they will change with volume. Examples of mixed costs include:

➤ Telephone expense—Basic monthly charge plus a cost per long-distance call

➤ Water—Basic monthly charge plus a cost per gallon

➤ Electricity—Basic usage charge plus additional costs for demand

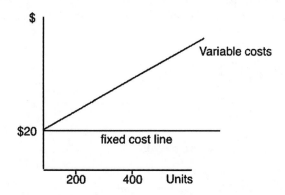

Again, *total* refers to units times dollars. For mixed costs, the expense totals are affected by the volume of the product or service you produce. Notice the fixed cost of $20 does not change with the increase in units. The variable cost does increase with volume, raising the total cost as units increase. If a company has several mixed costs, it is important to separate the fixed and variable costs from each other, particularly if the cost is significant.

Relevant Range

The relationship between variable cost, fixed cost, and volume will remain consistent within the *relevant range*. This is the range within which costs will react with volume in a consistent relationship. Beyond the upper and lower limits of this range, costs will not react in the same manner.

For example, rent expense is a fixed cost for a company producing 10,000 units. Beyond 10,000 units, the company will need additional space for production. This will require an additional cost. In the illustration that follows, the relevant range is 0 to 10,000 units. The cost is fixed at $800 for those required units. If the company produces more than 10,000 units, additional fixed costs will be required to produce more volume.

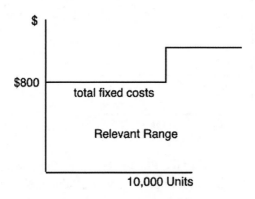

Cost Per Unit

Cost per unit is not the same as *total cost* for the number of units a company produces. Variable and fixed costs *per unit* will react much differently in relation to volume than *total* costs.

Variable Cost Per Unit

Ideally, variable cost per unit remains constant no matter how many units are produced. This is a justification for manufacturing plants to use a piece rate for direct labor employees.

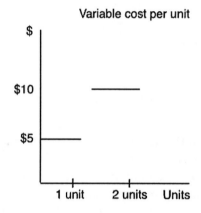

In this illustration, the variable cost per unit is $5. Two units cost $10 to produce. *Total* variable costs rise with the production of units but the cost *per unit* remains at $5.

Fixed Cost Per Unit

Fixed costs per unit will decrease as the production of units increase. This is logical, considering that total fixed costs do not change with the number of units produced. Projecting fixed cost per unit, however, is difficult without knowing the exact number of units to be produced.

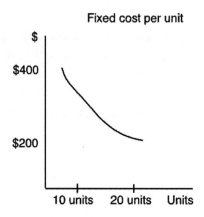

You might assume in looking at this illustration that cost per unit could continue down as long as you continued to produce more units. But there is a point where you reach maximum capacity and cannot reduce fixed cost per unit any further. To produce beyond maximum capacity, more equipment or a bigger building would be needed. At that point, the total fixed cost line would shift upward with the additional costs.

Cost Categories on the Income Statement

Each cost item on the Income Statement reacts differently to volume. It is important to isolate and separate the costs into fixed, variable, and mixed. But how do we know which costs are which? Remember, fixed costs are costs that do not move with increases or decreases in volume. And the following three-step process will lead you to determine which are variable and which are mixed:

Step 1: For each line item, determine the *basis*, the element on which the item is based. If wages are paid by the hour, for example, then the basis is the number of hours.

Step 2: Divide two different activity levels by the basis.

Step 3: If the quotient is the same for different activity levels, the cost is variable. If the quotient is different, then the item is a mixed cost.

Let's use the J.D. Lawn Service example to see how this works.

J.D. Lawn Service
Income Statement
For Months July, August, September

	July	August	Sept	
Revenue:				
Grass cutting	$12,000	$10,000	$15,000	
Expenses:				
Wage Expense	$ 4,800	$ 4,000	$ 6,000	Variable
Gasoline	480	400	600	Variable
Maintenance	96	80	120	Variable
Supplies	300	250	375	Variable
Truck Depreciation	400	400	400	Fixed
Equipment Depreciation	400	400	400	Fixed
Telephone Expense	86	84	92	Mixed
Advertising Expense	1,020	850	1,275	Variable
Administrative Services	340	340	340	Fixed
Utilities Expense	120	100	150	Variable
Rent Expense	800	800	800	Fixed
Miscellaneous Expense	600	500	750	Variable
Total Expenses	$ 9,442	$ 8,204	$11,302	
Net Income or (Net Loss)	$ 2,558	$ 1,796	$ 3,698	

As has been established, fixed costs are those that do not move with increases or decreases in volume. For the lawn service, you can see that truck and equipment depreciation are two costs that fit into this category. As the Income Statement shows, each of these expenses is $400 a month no matter what the volume.

Now let's look at variable and mixed costs for the lawn service.

Discerning Variable Costs

The J.D. Lawn Service Income Statement identifies the first two line items, wages and gasoline, as variable costs. Let's apply the three-step formula to see if this is correct.

Step 1: Determine the basis for each line item

Wage expense for J.D. Lawn Service is based on the number of hours, with the average lawn taking two hours to cut.

July: 120 lawns x 2 hours = 240 hours

August: 100 lawns x 2 hours = 200 hours

September: 150 lawns x 2 hours = 300 hours

Step 2: Divide two (or more) different levels of activity by the basis

In this case, the activity level being checked is the monthly wage expense. The wage expense for a given month is divided by the number of hours for that month, as follows:

$$\frac{\$4,800}{240 \text{ hours}} \qquad \frac{\$4,000}{200 \text{ hours}} \qquad \frac{\$6,000}{300 \text{ hours}}$$

Step 3: If the number is the same for both (or more) levels of activity, the cost is variable.

$$\frac{\$4,800}{240 \text{ hours}} = \$20 \qquad \frac{\$4,000}{200 \text{ hours}} = \$20 \qquad \frac{\$6,000}{300 \text{ hours}} = \$20$$

The number ($20) is the same for each level of activity. The cost is variable. Wage expense is pure variable cost. Wage expense increases and decreases depending on volume.

The same procedure will be used for each line item on the Income Statement.

	July	August	September
Gasoline	$480	$400	$600

For gasoline the basis is number of lawns: July 120; August 100; September 150. Dividing these numbers into the monthly gasoline figures results in a calculation of $4 per lawn—the same number for each level of activity. Gasoline is a variable cost.

Apply the same formula on other variable line items.

Discerning Mixed Costs

Mixed costs call for the same formula as variable costs. The difference comes out in Step 3. If the quotient is *different*, then the item is a mixed cost or is not purely variable. In the Income Statement for J.D. Lawn Service, telephone expense is marked as a mixed cost, with the following entries:

	July	August	September
Telephone Expense	$86	$84	$92

Let's apply the three-step formula to see if this is correct.

Step 1: Determine the basis for each line item

Telephone expense is based on the number of lawns:

July	August	September
120	100	150

Step 2: Divide two (or more) different levels of activity by the basis

$$\frac{\$86}{120} \qquad \frac{\$84}{100} \qquad \frac{\$92}{150}$$

0.72 0.84 0.61

Step 3: If the number is the same for both (or more) levels of activity, the cost is variable.

July		August	
$\dfrac{\$86}{100}$	=.86	$\dfrac{\$84}{120}$	=.70

Different quotients indicate the presence of fixed and mixed costs.

Further discovery of the telephone expense shows that $64 per month is a fixed charge and the reminder is variable. Thus, telephone expense must be separated into fixed and variable costs.

The intent of this quick exercise has been to look at the data to determine whether each line item was fixed or variable. But this analysis has not been very scientific. For example, wage expense in this exercise is variable because all of the workers are paid by the hour. This can be more complicated with different costs and with the additional information you would need to request in a real-life example.

P A R T 5

Controlling Costs

Contribution Margin on the Income Statement

A fundamental need in controlling costs is to understand what costs you can control. For the most part, variable costs can be controlled and fixed costs cannot. Thus, it is helpful to define all expenses as either variable or fixed. A simple traditional Income Statement may indicate on its list of expenses whether the cost is fixed or not, but the costs are not separated out on the statement itself, which looks like this:

	Sales
Less:	Expenses
=	Net Income or (Loss)

A traditional Income Statement for a retail company with merchandise would include the additional element of cost of goods sold, for a statement that looks like this:

	Sales
Less:	Cost of Goods Sold
=	Gross Profit (or Margin)
Less:	Expenses
=	Net Income or (Loss)

Again, this format does not separate fixed and variable expenses.

The *contribution margin* approach, however, separates all expenses into variable and fixed costs, as follows:

	Sales
Less:	Variable Expenses
=	**Contribution Margin**
Less:	Fixed Expenses
=	Net Income or (Loss)

Sales – Variable expenses = Contribution margin

This approach allows the manager to examine variable and fixed costs separately and determine their respective weights on net profits.

What follows is the J.D. Lawn Service Income Statement in the traditional format for July through September.

J.D. Lawn Service
Income Statement
For Months July, August, September

	July	August	September	Total
Revenue:				
Grass cutting	$12,000	$10,000	$15,000	$37,000
Expenses:				
Wage Expenses	$ 4,800	$ 4,000	$ 6,000	$14,800
Gasoline	480	400	600	1,480
Maintenance	96	80	120	296
Supplies	300	250	375	925
Truck Depreciation	400	400	400	1,200
Equipment Depreciation	400	400	400	1,200
Telephone Expense	86	84	92	262
Advertising Expense	1,020	850	1,275	3,145
Administrative Services	340	340	340	1,020
Utilities Expense	120	100	150	370
Rent Expense	800	800	800	2,400
Miscellaneous Expense	600	500	750	1,850
Total Expense	$ 9,442	$ 8,204	$11,302	$28,948
Net Income or (Net Loss)	$ 2,558	$ 1,796	$ 3,698	$ 8,052

The single list of expenses in this Income Statement does not provide an easy understanding of costs that can be controlled. Some are fixed and others are variable; some may be both. The better approach is to separate the costs.

In the income statement that follows, expenses are separated into variable and fixed costs. Costs that can be controlled (variable costs) are together above the contribution margin total, and noncontrollable costs (fixed costs) are below the contribution margin total.

J.D. Lawn Service
Income Statement
For Months July August September

	Total	
Revenue		
Grass cutting	$37,000	
Less: Variable Expenses		
Wage Expense	$14,800	
Gasoline	1,480	
Maintenance	296	
Supplies	925	Controllable Costs*
Advertising Expense	3,145	(variable costs)
Utilities Expense	370	
Miscellaneous Expense	1,850	
Telephone Expense	200	
Total Variable Expenses	$23,066	
Contribution Margin	$13,934	
Less: Fixed Expenses		
Truck Depreciation	1,200	
Equipment Depreciation	1,200	
Telephone Expense	62	Noncontrollable Costs
Administrative Services	1,020	(fixed costs)
Rent Expense	2,400	
Total Fixed Expenses	$ 5,882	
Net Income or (Net Loss)	$ 8,052	

*Controllable costs: Costs that management has the authority and ability to influence and change.

From this restatement of income, the ratio of variable to fixed costs is easily calculated. This gives an idea of the costs that can and cannot be controlled.

Variable costs are 79.68% of all expenses = $\dfrac{\$23{,}066}{\$28{,}948}$ Variable costs
Total expenses

Fixed costs are 20.32% of all expenses = $\dfrac{\$\ 5{,}882}{\$28{,}948}$ Fixed costs
Total expenses

In this illustration, 80% of expenses can be controlled. If sales shift downward by $1, then 80 cents (rounded) of the cost can be controlled and reduced to balance out a downturn in sales. The other 20% of the company's total costs, or 20 cents on every dollar (rounded), is, for the most part, fixed.

Activity-Based Costing

Accountants have used activity-based costing more and more in recent years. Managers should familiarize themselves with this term and its meaning.

Activity-based costing identifies all major operating activities manufacturing and non-manufacturing and allocates the costs for those activities to products and services that use the resources supplied by those activities.

Example: Purchasing Department costs $40,000
                      Activity 100,000 purchase orders   100,000

                                                                        = $.40 per purchase order

Activity-based costs are often targeted as an area for potential cost reduction. The larger the company, the more complex and obscure activity-based costs can be.

The fundamentals of activity-based costing are:

➤ Non-manufacturing and manufacturing costs may be assigned to a product or service. In traditional accounting only manufacturing costs would be assigned to the product. The sales department cost would be assigned to the product. Usually this is a period cost.

➤ Some manufacturing cost may not be assigned to the product. An example of this might be plant security personnel. These personnel costs are unaffected by the products being produced.

➤ Allocation of costs can be different. Companies could use departmental overhead rates rather than companywide rates.

➤ In traditional costing idle capacity (plant operations that were not used because of volume) would often be charged to the product. In activity costing only the amount of cost used from the plant would be allocated to the product.

Activity-based information is important to provide a "currency" for personnel that are not involved in the production, sale, or service of a product. Example: A salesperson hired at J.D. Lawn Service to make calls to prospective clients.

Salesperson cost $500 per week.= $125 per customer
                                    4 new customers

In many companies we can establish the activity or outcome and then determine the cost of that outcome. This gives management a quantitative number to determine whether a position really does increase net profits. These costs may not be easily discerned from financial statements.

Non-Value-Added Activity

It is important to understand that every activity in a company has an associated cost and that these activities may not add value to the product or service. An example of an activity cost in the J.D. Lawn Company is the movement of equipment to different lawn sites. This activity, while necessary, does not contribute revenue to the service. It would be important to look at a map of planned job sites to reduce travel time.

Other non-value-added activities would include:

> Product inspection

> Free delivery

> Storage

It is important to control costs. We should be able to identify costs and activities to better understand costs related to the production processes. Activities need to be value-added where possible. Other non-value added activities need to be reduced and contained.

Am I Breaking

Even?

The Cost-Volume-Profit Graph

"Am I breaking even?" is one of the fundamental questions in business. Every business needs to know the volume of business necessary to cover expenses. Activity in a business, if below break-even, will use up cash. Cash must then be replaced either through further investment or incurring debt.

The following graph illustrates the relationship among costs and revenue and break-even.

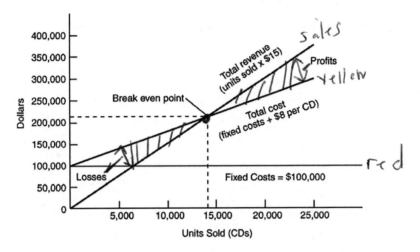

Total the variable costs and fixed costs, and where the sales line intersects with the total cost line, break-even will be calculated in units and dollars. This number represents the amount of money needed from revenue to cover total costs. The chart represents a simple approach to the solution.

Break-even in dollars   = Variable costs   + Fixed costs

A doctor might calculate how many patients she needs per hour to break-even. A retail store manager might wonder how many items are necessary to sell per day to break even. Finding this number will ensure better decisions. Let's illustrate how we find the break-even point using the J.D. Lawn Services.

It might seem easy to apply this formula to J.D. Lawn Services because the company's Income Statement already separates expenses into variable and fixed costs. If those two numbers were added together, that should be break-even.

$$\$28,948 \quad = \$23,066 \quad\quad + \$5,882$$

The problem with this approach is that J.D. Lawn Services produced a profit of $8,052. This means the variable costs of $23,066 are too high because they have contributed excess costs to reach a volume with $5,882 profit. The $28,948 figure is not break-even. It includes a profit of $8,052. Let's try a different method.

The Contribution Margin Approach to Break-Even

Before calculating the break-even, a few more pieces of information are needed.

➤ J.D has 15 commercial customers and charges them $100 per hour for lawn service.

➤ The average lawn takes two hours of time.

Since J.D. is using hourly rates, we are looking for the break-even in hours and dollars.

J.D. Lawn Service
Income Statement
For Months July, August, September

Revenue		Hourly rate	
Grass cutting	$37,000	$100.00 per hour	= 370 hours
Less: Total Variable Expenses	$23,066	$62.34 per hour	($23,066/370)
Contribution Margin	$13,934	= $37.66 per hour	
Less: Total Fixed Expenses	$5,882		
Net Income or (Net Loss)	$8,052		

Looking at this information:

$37,000 / 100 hours = 370 hours of cutting in three months

370 hours / 2 (average hours) = 185 lawns cut

What Is Break-Even in Hours?

Using the contribution margin method:

$$\frac{\text{Fixed cost}}{\text{CM per unit}} = \text{Break-even in hours}$$

Remember, over three months, J.D. had 370 hours of lawn-mowing activity. Break-even is 157 hours.

$$\frac{157 \text{ hours}}{2 \text{ hours}} = 79 \text{ lawns (rounded) in 3 months to break even}$$

J.D. Lawn had cut 185 lawns during this three-month period.

J.D. Lawn has a very good ratio of variable costs to fixed costs. A dry season of lawn cutting would still allow for a considerable drop in sales before the break-even point would be reached.

Calculating Break-Even in Dollars

There are two methods for calculating the break-even in dollars. The first calculates break-even by unit and multiplies the resulting unit by the unit rate. The second method uses fixed cost divided by the contribution margin as a percentage of total revenue.

Method 1

J.D. Lawn Service
Income Statement
For Months July, August, September

Revenue:		Hourly Rate
Grass cutting	$37,000	$100.00 per hour = 370 hours
Less: Total Variable Expenses	$23,066	- 62.34 per hour ($23,066/370)
Contribution Margin (CM)	$13,934	= $ 37.66
Less: Total Fixed Expenses	$ 5,882	
Net Income or (Net Loss)	$ 8,052	

$$\frac{\text{Fixed cost}}{\text{CM per unit}} = \text{Break-even in hours}$$

$$\frac{\$5,882}{= \$37.66} \quad 157 \text{ hours (rounded)}$$

After calculating the break-even in hours, just multiply it by the hourly rate.

157 hours x $100.00 per hour = $15,700

Method 2

Take the figures from the income statement and convert them to a percentage.

Revenue:

Grass cutting	$37,000	Always 100%	100%
Less: Total Variable Expenses	$23,066	23,066/37,000=	62%
Contribution Margin	$13,934	13,934/37,000=	38%
Less: Total Fixed Expenses	$5,882		
Net Income or (Net Loss)	$8,052		

$$\frac{\text{Fixed Costs}}{\text{Contribution Margin \%}} = \frac{\$5,882}{.38} = \$15,478 \text{ (difference due to rounding)}$$

Using both methods can provide verification of accuracy in your calculations.

Calculating "What If" Profit

Once you understand how to calculate break-even, then it is easy to calculate any volume necessary to reach a "target" profit.

To illustrate this point, let's say J.D. Lawn Service would like to generate a profit of $20,000.

Using the contribution margin formula, just add the desired profit to fixed cost:

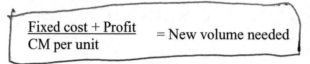

$$\frac{\text{Fixed cost} + \text{Profit}}{\text{CM per unit}} = \text{New volume needed}$$

J.D. Lawn Service
Income Statement
For Months July August September

Revenue		Hourly Rate
Grass cutting	$37,000	$100.00 per hour
Less: Total Variable Expenses	$23,066	-62.34 per hour
Contribution Margin	$13,934	= $ 37.66 per hour
Less: Total Fixed Expenses	$ 5,882	
Net Income or (Net Loss)	$ 8,052	

$$\frac{\text{Fixed cost} + \text{Profit}}{\text{CM per unit}} = \text{New volume needed}$$

$$\frac{\$5,882 + \$20,000}{\$37.66} \qquad 688 \text{ hours (rounded) or } 344 \text{ lawns}$$

Margin of Safety

The margin of safety is a measure of the difference between the actual level of sales and the break-even sales. It is the amount expressed in dollars, percentage, or units. When it is expressed as a percentage, the larger the ratio, the less risk to the company of not reaching the break-even.

J.D. Lawn Service
Income Statement
For Months July, August, September

Revenue:		Hourly Rate
Grass cutting	$37,000	$100.00 per hour
Less: Total Variable Expenses	$23,066	-62.34 per hour
Contribution Margin	$13,934	= $ 37.66 per hour
Less: Total Fixed Expenses	$ 5,882	
Net Income or (Net Loss)	$ 8,052	

$$\frac{\text{Actual Sales - Break-even Sales}}{\text{Actual Sales}} = \text{Margin of safety}$$

$$\frac{\$37,000 - \$15,700}{\$37,000} = 57.57\%$$

In dollars

$37,000 - $15,700 = $21,300

In Lawns cut

185 - 79 = 106

All of these numbers reflect the drop in volume to break-even.

PART 7

Operating

Leverage

66

Defining Operating Leverage

The term *operating leverage* refers to the percentage of fixed costs a company has on the income statement. The greater the amount of fixed costs, the greater the operating leverage. The degree of operating leverage indicates how sensitive the company is to sales increases and decreases.

For J.D. Lawn Service, the fixed costs are not high in relation to the variable costs.

J.D. Lawn Service
Income Statement
For Months July, August, September

Revenue Grass cutting	$37,000	
Less: Total Variable Expenses	$23,066	79.68% Variable costs
Contribution Margin	**$13,934**	
Less: Total Fixed Expenses	$ 5,882	20.32% Fixed costs
Net Income or (Net Loss)	**$ 8,052**	

The computation for the degree of operating leverage is:

$$\text{Degree of Operating Leverage} = \frac{\text{Contribution Margin}}{\text{Net Income}}$$

$$\text{Degree of Operating Leverage} = \frac{\$13,934}{\$ 8,052}$$

$$\text{Degree of Operating Leverage} = 1.73$$

If J.D. Lawn sales increased by 25%, the net income of the company would increase:

Net income increase =	Operating Leverage	x	Percent of sales increase
43.3% =	1.73	x	25%

The same thing would happen if J.D. were to see a *decrease* of 25% in sales: The company's income would *decline* by 43.3%.

Operating Leverage and the Bottom Line

What is important about operating leverage is that the impact on the "bottom line" decreases as a company moves further away from the break-even point.

J.D. Lawn Service
Income Statement
For Months July, August, September

		Proposed
Revenue: Grass cutting	$37,000	$50,000
Less: Total Variable Expenses	$23,066	$31,170
Contribution Margin	$13,934	$18,830
Less: Total Fixed Expenses	$ 5,882	$ 5,882
Net Income or (Net Loss)	$ 8,052	$13,948
Operating Leverage	$13,934	$18,830
	$ 8,052	$12,948
=	1.73	1.45

If J.D. Lawn makes $50,000 in revenue such that profit becomes $12,948, the company has moved further away from break-even. Operating leverage has been reduced.

Although this is important, it is even more important to look at the ratio of fixed and variable costs. The next illustration will show what can happen when a company has a very high degree of operating leverage due to high fixed costs.

Let's exchange the variable and fixed costs of J.D. Lawn Service. The example on the left below uses the same numbers for the company. For the example on the right, the fixed and variable numbers have been switched to give J.D. more fixed costs and less variable costs. This will create a more dynamic change in operating leverage. Notice that in both scenarios, the company still has the same sales and net income figures.

J.D. Lawn Service
Income Statement
For Months July, August, September

	J.D. has high variable costs and low fixed costs	J.D. has low variable and high fixed costs
Revenue		
Grass cutting	$37,000	$37,000
Less: Total Variable Expenses	**$23,066**	**$ 5,882**
Contribution Margin	$13,934	$31,118
Less: Total Fixed Expenses	**$ 5,882**	**$23,066**
Net Income or (Net Loss)	$ 8,052	$ 8,052
Operating Leverage	= $13,934	$31,118
	$ 8,052	$ 8,052
	= 1.73	3.86

A decrease of 10% in sales would result in a 17.3 percent drop in net income where variable costs are high. A decrease of 10% in sales would result in a 38.6% change in net income if J.D. had high fixed costs.

This concept is important because it illustrates the problems that can occur with large fixed costs. Of course with an increase in sales, the "bottom line" would improve dramatically. The lesson here is that companies with a high ratio of fixed to variable costs must be very careful of decreases in volume.

Influences on

Pricing

Pricing in Line with the Competition

Most companies must keep an eye on the competition. If a rival firm reduces prices, you may need to do the same or lose market share. Yet it is important to remember that you cannot be at the mercy of your "dumbest" competitor. Continuing to lower selling price will result in lower profit margins. This is not a long-term strategy that most companies can continue. Weathering a price war requires cash reserves, so some companies will be driven out of business.

Examples of this can be found throughout business history. The video rental business suffered through a period of increased competition and the lowering of prices to 99 cents for overnight rentals. At that price point many stores found themselves at break-even or below. After the shakeout and loss of numerous small businesses, both the price and profits returned to industry norms.

It is important to understand your costs and strategy. A customer focus will aid you in determining what defensive and offensive moves are required to combat competitive pricing moves.

Trade-Offs Between Price and Demand

Should you set prices high to make more money on each unit sold, or should you set prices low and make up the difference in volume? Such are the trade-offs between higher prices and increased volume.

Demand has to be very strong to increase selling price and not lose volume. There are two strategies to pricing in relation to demand: skimming the market and penetrating the market.

Skimming the Market

Skimming the market is used by companies that enter a market with a new product or by companies that enjoy little competition for very high quality products or services.

Such companies set prices high to cover costs and ensure profits after recouping research and development costs.

Skimming the Market

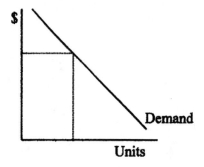

Skimming the market produces a lower demand for units. If profit margins are high and the number of customers is sufficient, this can be a permanent pricing strategy. Many luxury products pursue this strategy.

Penetrating the Market

The pricing strategy of penetrating the market uses a lower price to increase volume and gain an advantage by taking as much market as possible quickly. Many Internet companies in 2000 and 2001 that filed for bankruptcy had used just such a strategy to gain market share.

The problem with this strategy is that profit margins are thin or nonexistent. Sudden changes in the market can result in fewer sales, a drop below break-even based on volume, and a sudden loss of cash flow. If companies have a high degree of operating leverage, this can produce sudden death for the organization.

Penetration Pricing

Setting the price for a product or service is an extremely important management decision. Set the price too low and a company may not meet profit expectations.

A case in point was a new fitness facility that, once completed, failed to set its price to reflect current conditions. Underpricing memberships resulted in turning away customers because of demand and limited capacity. The business struggled to break even the first year of operation. It was forced to increase fees the second year, causing many members to resign.

While offering very low pricing initially works to attract customers to a new business, it is difficult to raise a price significantly in a short period without customer reaction. Had the initial discount been lower, the required increase might have been less objectionable.

Elasticity of Demand Illustrated

Demand that is elastic will increase or decrease with price. The amount of increase or decrease is often difficult to determine. Quantitative models will aid in this decision but assumptions may not always come true.

The following chart shows how changes in price affect volume. Demand that is elastic changes with volume. Demand that is inelastic changes little. Statistical models help to determine these changes in quantity and price. Further study will provide more information.

Quantity x	Unit Sales Price	= Total Revenue per month	- Total Cost per month	= Profit or Loss
20	$75	$1,500	$2,500	($1,000)
40	$70	$2,800	$3,000	($ 200)
60	$65	$3,900	$3,500	$ 400
65	$60	$3,900	$3,600	$ 300
70	$55	$3,850	$3,800	$ 50
75	$50	$3,750	$3,750	($ 200)

The horizontal line in this example illustrates the point at which a company can *maximize profit* based on elastic demand. Research needs to be done before changing price. Markets and consumers do not always react as predicted. Many decisions determining the outcome of price reductions or increases cannot be applied with certainty. The results will come about from historical and statistical models.

Market and Cost Influences on Pricing

In most industries there are market and cost influences on pricing. It is good to understand how much influence each has on your pricing strategy. Unfortunately, the market is not always willing to pay the price necessary to cover your costs and desired profit. More often, it is necessary to contain the costs and/or revise profit expectations to produce at the price the market is willing to pay.

In agriculture, for example, the price of products is determined by the marketplace. To make a profit, a farmer must produce below the market price. There are often periods when costs cannot be contained, and losses result from a decrease in market prices. This leads farmers to become more efficient and effective in their production techniques.

Constraints from customers and competitors force businesses to apply the same production principles used in agriculture. To survive a company will look to efficiency and effectiveness when price alone cannot increase profits or market share.

Qualitative Factors in Relation to Price

Some companies provide a product with market differential—a niche—where qualitative factors such as prestige, image, and belonging add to the ability to focus more on customer needs and less on price.

This is where branding plays an important part in conveying a message consistent with your image. If you are able to establish a strong, positive brand identity, many customers will pay more for that brand, even if the actual product is practically identical to "Brand X."

Price is always an important consideration. Some companies enjoy little competition and provide high-end products. And some direct marketing companies control growth by increasing price to reduce demand. We would all like to be in that position. For most of us this is not the case.

Making the
Numbers
Work for You

Responsible Decision-Making

To make responsible decisions, a great amount of data must be collected during the problem-solving phase. And the relevant information must be separated from the irrelevant. Two irrelevant costs are *sunk costs*, costs incurred yesterday, and *common costs*—costs that are the same for all alternatives under consideration.

The impact on profit is one of the most important issues for a company. The effect on income involves cost and revenue decisions. *Relevant* revenue and cost can be defined as *numbers that change as a result of a decision*.

The following process can help make identifying relevant costs more effective. An illustration of the process can also be found on the next page.

> **Identify all costs**

> **Eliminate costs that cannot be changed**

> Examples of these costs include lease payments for machinery, depreciation expense for assets previously purchased, interest payments on existing debt, etc.

> **Eliminate costs that do not change between the alternatives under consideration**

> This will vary depending on the decision to be made. For example, if the decision is between parts suppliers, and labor will be the same using either part, labor can be eliminated as a relevant cost.

The costs that remain are required for the decision. Some of these costs still may not be relevant. Further cost analysis will be required after all the data has been collected, the irrelevant data discarded, and costs looked at once more to make sure this data is necessary. The more important and costly the decision, the more time and analysis should be directed toward the differing outcomes.

These four dollar signs represent all costs

Common Costs

**These three remaining signs represent costs that do differ
between alternatives**

Unnecessary
Costs

These two signs represent costs that are necessary to the decision

 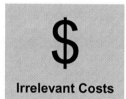

Irrelevant Costs

The remaining costs are relevant to the decision

Quality Management

There are costs associated with quality. Low-quality products lead to higher warranty costs and unhappy customers. This in turn leads to a poor reputation for the company.

Quality costs can be classified into four groups.

Prevention costs	*Activities that reduce defects during the production process*
Appraisal costs	*Activities that identify defective products (inspection)*
Internal failure	*Identifying bad parts during process or inspection*
External failure	*Customer identifies the defect or the company recalls the product*

Quality cost information will help a company determine the size of quality issues, the costs to resolve those issues, and a better focus on the issues. Quality is an important component to costing. Remember, you can produce the best product or service in the world but you cannot let the benefit outweigh the price the customer can pay for the product or service. Companies must look at the customers they serve, and then deliver a quality product or service these customers can afford.

APPENDIX

Review of the Numbers

We have covered many areas of cost-related functions in this book. Let's review the basics:

Accurate and Consistent Information

Recording financial information must be done consistently. Comparing records over time requires data to be historically correct and recorded in the same accounts and categories. Failure to do so creates the inability to compare and contrast financial information.

Financial Statement Analysis

Managers need to have a greater understanding of the financial statements a company uses for external and internal reporting. The numbers should be studied and relationships among statements established.

Cost Categories

Reviewing definitions and explanations of the five cost categories will serve you well when discussing and analyzing internal financial reporting in your organization. Remember that all costs, and allocation of those costs to products and services, are required to review pricing.

Cost Behavior

It is important in every organization to learn the impact of volume on individual costs and how those costs behave related to various levels of production. This ability to identify costs and control them will aid in maximizing profits and in providing more efficiency and effectiveness in the production processes.

Break-Even Analysis

This concept is critical for many small businesses and provides large companies with many divisions and product lines the ability to examine fixed and variable costs critically. For many companies, the ability to know how much product or service must be sold on a yearly, monthly, weekly, daily, and perhaps hourly basis is critical for survival. It also strengthens marketing efforts and cost controls.

Operating Leverage

Understanding the importance of fixed and variable costs to the "bottom line" is essential for all operations personnel. The degree of leverage a company has will influence decisions when selling prices and volume begin to fluctuate. Understanding how these costs affect your company will be the difference in making high profits or high losses. Responsiveness to sales fluctuation cannot be understated when a company has a high degree of operating leverage.

Price

Price and its relationship to the customer and competition are very important. Competing on price alone is a strategy followed by many companies in every segment of business. It is important to determine if this will be long- or short-term advantage for your company. You must understand customer demand and customer perception of the products and services you sell.

Decision-Making

The constraint of financial resources will influence all decisions made in an organization. The importance of relevant data to get to the "right decisions" cannot be ignored. The numbers can prove whatever you want them to prove in many decisions. We must resist the temptation to use only the financial information that makes our point. The long-term health of any business is predicated on sound decision-making. We have seen the results of decisions that create short-term gains at the expense of long-term survival. We must exercise caution when using numbers. Remember, management's responsibility should be to the long-range survivability of the company. Other objectives should include the ability to control resources and provide products and services to customers. There should also be a sense of responsibility to the financial well-being of the workers who have made your company grow. The wealth created through prudent financial management can provide for the well-being of all that contribute to the company. This is a large task. *Accounting Essentials* will help get you there.

I hope this book has been a useful tool for you. Please feel free to e-mail me at jayjacquet@hotmail.com. Your comments and suggestions would be appreciated.

Appendix to Part 2

Self-Help Test

Record the transactions with a + or – under each of categories listed below:

1. Invested $20,000 in the business
2. Sold $1,000 on account A R
3. Paid wages of $850
4. Purchased a truck for $10,000 cash
5. Purchased $500 of inventory on credit
6. Sold $6,000 on account A R
7. Received a telephone bill for $250 A P
8. Paid the rent, $300
9. Withdrew cash for personal use, $250
10. Invested a used truck in the business $3,500

	Assets	Liabilities	Owner's Equity	Revenue	Expenses
1.	+20,000		+20,000		
2.	1,000			1,000	
3.	−850				− 850
4.	−10,000 +10,000				
5.	+500	+500			
6.	+6,000			+6,000	
7.		+250			
8.	−300				−300
9.	−250	−250	−250		
10.	+3,500	+3,500	+3,500		
	$29,600	$750	$23,250 +$5,600 $28,850	$7,000	$1,400 In come $5,600

Self-Help Test Solution

Record the transactions with a + or – under each of categories listed below:

1. Invested $20,000 in the business
2. Sold $1,000 on account
3. Paid wages of $850
4. Purchased a truck for $10,000 cash
5. Purchased $500 of inventory on credit
6. Sold $6,000 on account
7. Received a telephone bill for $250
8. Paid the rent, $300
9. Withdrew cash for personal use, $250
10. Invested a used truck in the business, $3,500

	Assets	Liabilities	Owner's Equity	Revenue	Expenses
1.	+20,000		+20,000		
2.	+1,000			+1,000	←
3.	-850				-850
4.	-10,000 +10,000				
5.	+500	+500			
6.	+6,000			+6,000	
7.		+250			-250
8.	-300				-300
9.	-250		-250		
10.	+3,500		+3,500		

Assets		Liabilities		Owner's Equity	Revenue	- Expense = Profit
$29,600	=	$750	+	$23,250	$7,000	- $1,400 = $5,600
				5,600 ←		
				$28,850		

Appendix to Part 3

Self-Help Test 1

Manufacturing or non-manufacturing costs

Classify the following costs as manufacturing (M) or non-manufacturing (N).

M   1. Factory supplies

M   2. Cost of a machine breakdown

N   3. Legal expenses

N   4. Salesman commission

M   5. Payroll taxes — factory

N   6. Payroll taxes — marketing department

N   7. Advertising

M   8. Factory rent

Manufacturing

Factory supplies
Cost of a machine breakdown
Payrol taxes - factory
Factory rent

Non-manufacturing

legal expense
Salesmen commision
Payroll taxes- marketing
Advertising

Self-Help Test 1 Solution

Manufacturing or non-manufacturing costs

Classify the following costs as manufacturing (M) or non-manufacturing (N).

M   1. Factory supplies

M   2. Cost of a machine breakdown

N   3. Legal expenses

N   4. Salesperson commission

M   5. Payroll taxes — factory

N   6. Payroll taxes — marketing department

N   7. Advertising

M   8. Factory rent

Self-Help Test 2

Traceable costs

Classify the following costs as indirect (I) or direct (D)

_I_ 1. Depreciation of factory equipment

_I_ 2. Janitorial supplies

_D_ 3. Glue used in the making of furniture

_I_ 4. Fringe benefits (sick leave)

_I_ 5. Oil for machinery

_I_ 6. Foreman's salary

_D_ 7. Tires used in the making of bikes

_D_ 8. Direct labor

Indirect

Depreciation of factory equipment
Janitorial supplies
Fringe benefits (sick leave)
oil for machinery
Foreman's salary

Direct

Glue used in making of furniture
tires used in making of bikes
Direct Labor

Self-Help Test 2 Solution

Traceable costs

Classify the following costs as indirect (I) or direct (D)

I   1. Depreciation of factory equipment

I   2. Janitorial supplies

D   3. Glue used in the making of furniture

I   4. Fringe benefits (sick leave)

I   5. Oil for machinery

I   6. Foreman's salary

D   7. Tires used in the making of bikes

D   8. Direct labor

Self-Help Test 3

Timing costs

Classify the following costs as product costs (P) or period costs (C).

P 1. Wood used in the making of furniture.

C 2. Travel expense

P 3. Overtime labor

C 4. Legal fees

P 5. Rework of bad parts

P 6. Worker's compensation

C 7. Marketing expense

C 8. Administrative expense

<u>Product Costs</u>

Wood used in making of furniture
Overtime labor
rework of bad parts
Workers Compensation

<u>Period Costs</u>

Travel expense
Legal fees
Marketing expense
Administrative expense

Self-Help Test 3 Solution

Timing costs

Classify the following costs as product costs (P) or period costs (C).

P   1. Wood used in the making of furniture.

C   2. Travel expense

P   3. Overtime labor

C   4. Legal fees

P   5. Rework of bad parts

P   6. Worker's compensation

C   7. Marketing expense

C   8. Administrative expense

Self-Help Test 4

Place a (V) for variable or a (F) for fixed costs.

The following costs are associated with a factory operation

V   1. Electricity used by the machines

F   2. Rent on a factory building

V   3. Hourly wage workers

F   4. Factory manager salary

V   5. Lubricants needed for machines

F   6. Property taxes on factory

F   7. Depreciation on equipment

V   8. Material used in the production process

Variable

electricity used by the machines
Hourly wage workers
lubricents needed for machines
material used in production process

Fixed

rent on a factory building
factory manager salary
property - taxes - factory
Depreciation on equipment

Self-Help Test 4 Solution

Place a (V) for variable or a (F) for fixed costs.

The following costs are associated with a factory operation

V   1. Electricity used by the machines

F   2. Rent on a factory building

V   3. Hourly wage workers

F   4. Factory manager salary

V   5. Lubricants needed for machines

F   6. Property taxes on factory

F   7. Depreciation on equipment

V   8. Material used in the production process

Appendix to Part 4

Self-Help Test 1

The following is a list of various costs of producing shirts. Classify each cost as variable (V), fixed (F) or mixed (M).

_V_ 1. Lubricants used to oil machinery

_F_ 2. Janitorial costs of $3,000 per month.

_F_ 3. Salary of production foreman

_V_ 4. Hourly wages of sewing operators

_M_ 5. Telephone bills of $59.00 per month and $.10 per minute

_M_ 6. Advertising costs

_F_ 7. Depreciation on equipment

_V_ 8. Electric costs $.015 per kilowatt-hour

_V_ 9. Cloth used in production

_F_ 10. Maintenance contract of $10,000 per year on equipment

fixed
Janitorial Costs of $3,000 a month
Salary of production foreman
Depreciation on equipment
Maintenance contract of $10,000 per year on equipment

Variable
Lubricants used to oil machinery
Hourly wages of sewing operators
electric costs $0.015 per kilowatt-hr
cloth used in production

Mixed
Advertising costs
telephone bills $59 per month per and $0.10 minute

Self-Help Test 1 Solution

The following is a list of various costs of producing shirts. Classify each cost as variable (V), fixed (F) or mixed (M).

V   1. Lubricants used to oil machinery

F   2. Janitorial costs of $3,000 per month.

F   3. Salary of production foreman

V   4. Hourly wages of sewing operators

M   5. Telephone bills of $59.00 per month and $.10 per minute

M   6. Advertising costs

F   7. Depreciation on equipment

V   8. Electric costs $.015 per kilowatt-hour

V   9. Cloth used in production

F   10. Maintenance contract of $10,000 per year on equipment

Self-Help Test 2

The Pen Company produces ink pens within a relevant range of production of 10,000 to 30,000 pens per year. Complete the following cost schedule using the information provided below.

Number of pens produced

	10,000	20,000	30,000
Total Costs:			
Total variable costs	$ 9,000	(1) 18,000	(2) 27,000
Total fixed costs	18,000	(3) 18,000	(4) 18,000
Total costs	$27,000	36,000	45,000
Cost per unit:			
Variable cost per unit	(5) 0.9	(6) 0.9	(7) 0.9
Fixed cost per unit	(8) 1.8	(9) 0.9	(10) 0.6
Total cost per unit	(11) 2.7	(12) 1.8	(13) 1.5

Δ 0.9   Δ 0.3

Self-Help Test 2 Solution

The Pen Company produces ink pens within a relevant range of production of 10,000 to 30,000 pens per year. Complete the following cost schedule using the information provided below.

	Number of pens produced		
	10,000	**20,000**	**30,000**
Total Costs:			
Total variable costs	$ 9,000	$18,000	$27,000
Total fixed costs	18,000	18,000	18,000
Total costs	$27,000	$36,000	$45,000
Cost per unit:			
Variable cost per unit	$ .90	$ .90	$ .90
Fixed cost per unit	-1.80	.90	.60
Total cost per unit	$2.70	$1.80	$1.50

Note: Variable cost per unit does not change with volume

Fixed cost per unit decreases with volume

Total costs at the top of the page are divided by number of pens to get cost per unit.

Appendix to Part 6

Self-Help Test 1

The Cookie Company has developed deluxe cookies. The company sells one box for $20. The company sold 15,000 boxes of cookies this year. Fixed costs were $182,000 and variable costs were $6 per box. What is the number of boxes necessary to break even?

$(15,000) \ \$20 = \$300,000$ revenue

price 20

V C $\frac{6}{14}$ $\frac{182,000}{14} = \$13,000$ boxes $\$13,000$ boxes

$\$182,000 + \$6(15,000) = 272,000$

2,000 boxes × 20 = $\$40,000$ profit

Self-Help Test 2

Bob has a car wash and charges $3 to wash a car. The variable cost of washing the car is $1 and fixed costs per year are $15,000. How many cars need to be washed to break even?

$3 - 1 = 2 \ (cm)$

$\frac{15,000}{2} = \$7,500$ car washer

$\$7$

7,500 car washes needed to break even

Self-Help Test 3

Betty has a shoe shop. The average sales price for a pair of shoes is $60. Variable costs are $20 per pair. Fixed expenses are $400,000. Calculate the annual shop sales required if Betty wants to make $20,000 in profit.

$60 - 20 = 40$

$\frac{400,000}{40} = 10,000$ pair of shoes to break even

$\frac{\$400,000 + \$20,000}{40} = 10,500$ pair of shoes

need sell 500 more pair of shoes

Self-Help Test 1 Solution

The Cookie Company has developed deluxe cookies. The company sells one box for $20. The company sold 15,000 boxes of cookies this year. Fixed costs were $182,000 and variable costs were $6 per box. What is the number of boxes necessary to break even?

Sales	$20
Variable cost	6
Contribution margin	$14

$$\frac{\text{Fixed cost}}{\text{CM}} \qquad \frac{\$182,000}{\$14} = 13,000 \text{ Boxes to break-even}$$

Self-Help Test 2 Solution

Bob has a car wash and charges $3 to wash a car. The variable cost of washing the car is $1 and fixed costs per year are $15,000. How many cars need to be washed to break even?

Sales	$3.00
Variable cost	1.00
Contribution margin	$2.00

$$\frac{\text{Fixed cost}}{\text{CM}} \qquad \frac{\$15,000}{\$2.00} = 7,500 \text{ Cars to break-even}$$

Self-Help Test 3 Solution

Betty has a shoe shop. The average sales price for a pair of shoes is $60. Variable costs are $20 per pair. Fixed expenses are $400,000. Calculate the annual shop sales required if Betty wants to make $20,000 in profit.

Sales	$60
Variable cost	20
Contribution margin	$40

$$\frac{\text{Fixed cost} + \text{Profit}}{\text{CM}} \qquad \frac{\$400,000 + \$20,000}{\$40} = 10,500 \text{ Shoes}$$

Appendix to Part 7

Self-Help Test 1

Operating Leverage Degree of Operating leverage = 6

JL Inc. has developed a new environmental board game. The company sold 35,000 games last year. The selling price was $15 per game. Fixed costs for the game last year were $350,000 and variable costs were $3 per game. Calculate the degree of operating leverage for the company.

CM 15-3 = $12 per gem.

Break even 29,166 units
profit 5834 units

$2 $ game profit

Sales 35,000 ($15) = $525,000
var (35,000) (3) = $105,000

CM $420,000
fixed $350,000
Income $70,000

Degree
Operating Leverage $\left(\dfrac{420,000}{7,000}\right) = 6$

Self-Help Test 2

JL Inc. can produce three times the number of boards next year (105,000). The company selling price will continue to be $15 per game. Variable costs will be reduced by 20% with the purchase of automated equipment. The new fixed costs for the year are $800,000. Calculate the degree of operating leverage for the company.

Sales $15 (105,000) = 1,875,000   3 × .2 = 0.6

Variable 24 (105,00) 282,000

CM 1,323,000

fixed 800,000

Income 523,000

$\dfrac{1,323,000}{523,000} = 2.53$ degree of operating leverage

Self-Help Test 1 Solution

Operating Leverage

JL Inc. has developed a new environmental board game. The company sold 35,000 games last year. The selling price was $15 per game. Fixed costs for the game last year were $350,000 and variable costs were $3 per game. Calculate the degree of operating leverage for the company.

Sales	35,000 x $15	= $525,000
Variable costs	35,000 x $3	= 105,000
Contribution Margin		420,000
Fixed costs		350,000
Net Income		$ 70,000
Operating Leverage	=	$420,000
		$70,000
		= 6

Self-Help Test 2 Solution

JL Inc. can produce three times the number of boards next year (105,000). The company selling price will continue to be $15 per game. Variable costs will be reduced by 20% with the purchase of automated equipment. The new fixed costs for the year are $800,000. Calculate the degree of operating leverage for the company.

Sales	105,000 x $15	= $1,575,000
Variable costs	105,000 x $2.40	= 252,000
Contribution Margin		1,323,000
Fixed costs		800,000
Net Income		$ 523,000
Operating Leverage	=	$1,323,000
		$ 523,000
		= 2.53

Additional Reading

Dickey, Terry. *Basics of Budgeting.* 1992.

Gill, James O. and Moira Chatton. *Financial Analysis.*2001.

Gill, James O. and Moira Chatton. *Understanding Financial Statements.* 1999.

Jacquet, Jay L. and William C. Miller, Jr. *The Accounting Cycle.* 2002.

Truchon, Richard P. *Basic Business Math.* 1997.

NOTES

NOTES

NOTES

NOTES

Also Available

Subject Areas Include:

Accounting & Finance

Business Ethics

Business Skills

Communication

Customer Service

Design

Diversity in Business

Human Resources & Leveraging Your People

Jobs & Careers

Management & Leadership

Operations

Product Development & Marketing

Sales Coaching & Prospecting

Women in Leadership

Writing & Editing

AX156052698X
ISBN-13 978-1-56052-698-8
ISBN-10 1-56052-698-X